altered photo
ARTISTRY

Turn Everyday Images into Works of Art on Fabric

BETH WHEELER
with LORI MARQUETTE

C&T PUBLISHING

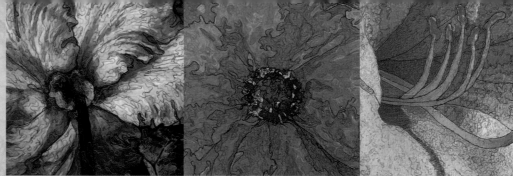

Text copyright © 2007 by Beth Wheeler

Art copyright © 2007 by Beth Wheeler & C&T Publishing, Inc.

Publisher: Amy Marson

Editorial Director: Gailen Runge

Acquisitions Editor: Jan Grigsby

Editor: Kesel Wilson

Technical Editors: Wendy Mathson and Carolyn Aune

Copyeditor/Proofreader: Wordfirm Inc.

Design Director/Cover & Book Designer: Christina D. Jarumay

Photographers: Joshua A. Mulks & Luke Mulks

Production Coordinator: Kirstie L. Pettersen

Illustrator: Wendy Mathson

Photography by C&T Publishing, Inc., unless otherwise noted

Published by C&T Publishing, Inc., P.O. Box 1456, Lafayette, CA 94549

Library of Congress Cataloging-in-Publication Data

Wheeler, Beth Schwartz.

  Altered photo artistry : turn everyday images into works of art on fabric / Beth Wheeler with Lori Marquette.

    p. cm.

  Includes bibliographical references.

  ISBN-13: 978-1-57120-440-0 (paper trade : alk. paper)

  ISBN-10: 1-57120-440-7 (paper trade : alk. paper)

  1. Textile crafts. 2. Photographs on cloth. 3. Computer art. I. Marquette, Lori II. Title.

TT699.W45 2007

746--dc22

                              2007006767

Printed in China

9 8 7 6 5 4 3 2 1

table of

contents

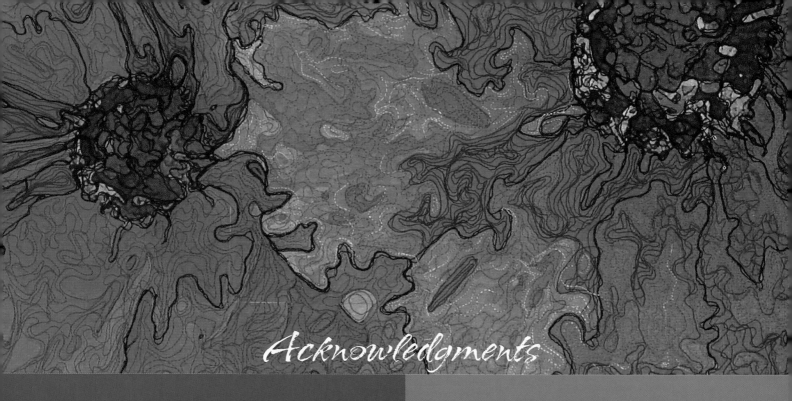

Acknowledgments

From Beth

I'd like to thank the following individuals for their help and support:

Geoffrey Wheeler, my wonderful husband, who loves me every day, regardless of crazy deadlines.

Eleanor Ferguson, who first introduced me to the world of needlework. Thanks, Mom, for putting my very first crocheted chain on the Christmas tree. It meant so much to a six-year-old.

Walter Johnson, the best dad ever! The one who told me to reach for the stars—and that there is no such word as *can't*, only *won't*. I miss you every day, Dad!

Jake Schwartz, the son who brings me joy daily with a quip, a grin, or a comment, and who offers a unique vision of life through his incredible poetry.

Lori Marquette, who talks me off the ledge on a regular basis. I couldn't do this without you!

The creative, enthusiastic family at C&T Publishing—especially Jan Grigsby, our guardian angel.

Thank you. I am so grateful to have you all in my life!

"In all your ways acknowledge Him and He will direct your paths." Proverbs 3:6

From Lori

My thanks go to the many friends and family members who have loved and supported me, especially the following:

Tyler and Ryan Marquette, my two sons—the ultimate joys of my life!

David and Judy Gorrell, the best parents ever! Thank you for your unending love and support.

Marcelene Gorrell, my beloved grandmother, who always believed in me and taught me more than she could ever imagine.

Beth Shan Wheeler, my best friend, who enables me to find the courage to step outside my creative box and discover new adventures. Thanks, Sipster!

Pammy Sue, you have been through a lot with us…and I know most of it's our fault! Thanks for your willingness, encouragement, and patience!

"Whatever you do, whether in word or deed, do it all in the name of the Lord Jesus, giving thanks to God the Father through Him." Colossians 3:17

introduction

*A*LTERED PHOTO ARTISTRY REPRESENTS A COMBINATION OF TECHNIQUES FAMILIAR TO MANY QUILT ARTISTS. IT COMBINES PHOTOGRAPHY, IMAGE MANIPULATION, PRINTING ON FABRIC, AND FREE-MOTION QUILTING TO CREATE TRULY UNIQUE IMAGES OF EXTRAORDINARY BEAUTY.

The art of printing on fabric has been evolving for decades. From silk-screening to photo transfer to direct printing, each advance was innovative at its introduction and is still popular today for certain applications. The ultimate test of any technique, however, is its ability to provide durable, true-color reproduction without changing the hand (drape and texture) of the fabric.

With computer technology advancing at the speed of light and the incorporation of that technology into various textile-based industries, we are able to take the awesome concept of printing on fabric and apply it in our homes and studios as well. Art quilters and textile artists alike are moving outside the box and stepping into ever-more exploratory expressions of art.

The techniques presented in this book afford the artist an opportunity to use computer, printer, fabric, and thread as artistic tools to add texture, dimension, and definition to images printed on fabric. The process is relatively simple, the results are fabulous, and finished pieces are easily recognized as the fine art they are.

We strive to provide the reader with information about tools, materials, computers, and digital equipment, plus tips and techniques to inspire. As you explore our techniques, we hope you add personal touches to the steps and take the techniques to new heights.

The Fundamentals

By the time you finish reading and using this book, you too will be able to create works of art that begin as simple photos and end as wonderfully thread-embellished, quilted masterpieces.

We walk you step-by-step through the equipment and software you'll need to take your own photos and apply enhancement and artistic alteration to them. We demonstrate how to print these images on pretreated fabric at various sizes and how to beautifully and strikingly embellish them with thread. And finally, we show you how to incorporate these pieces of art into quilts, larger fabric projects, or simply frame and hang them as their own unique creations.

Enjoy the adventure!

Beth and Lori

photography
equipment
& supplies

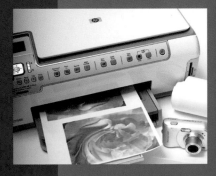

*W*ITH JUST A FEW PIECES OF EQUIPMENT, YOU CAN BEGIN PRINTING IMAGES ON FABRIC RIGHT AT HOME. IN THIS CHAPTER, WE'LL GUIDE YOU THROUGH CHOOSING PRETREATED FABRICS, INKJET PRINTERS, INKS, COMPUTERS, SCANNERS, AND DIGITAL CAMERAS. WE'LL ALSO GIVE YOU A QUICK OVERVIEW OF THE TYPES OF PHOTO-EDITING SOFTWARE AND FREE, DIGITAL ART AVAILABLE TO YOU.

Pretreated Fabrics

Pretreated fabrics make it easy to print photos and artwork on fabric at home. If you can print it on paper, you can print it on fabric!

There are several brands of pretreated inkjet fabrics on the market, but they all work in a similar manner. The fabric is coated with fixative that holds the ink on the fibers and has a paper or Mylar backing that stabilizes the fabric as it travels through the printer.

These pretreated fabrics are available in a variety of sizes and fabric types. They can be purchased in packs of 8½″ × 11″ sheets or as rolls that vary in width from 8½″ to 60″. The width of your printer will dictate which size you choose. Fabric types available include 100% cotton poplin, 100% cotton twill, 100% cotton canvas, cotton denim, linen, silk habotai, silk georgette, silk dupioni, and organza. This variety allows you to choose the fabric appropriate for your specific project.

- Poplin is a high-thread-count fabric that blends well with commercially printed quilting cottons and dress-making fabrics.

- Twill is a little heavier and very durable—perfect for purses, pillows, tote bags, or anything that will receive a lot of stitching and wear.

- Canvas is an interesting fabric. If you print a photograph on it, it looks like artist's canvas. If you print artwork on it and add embroidery stitches by hand or machine, it looks like needlework fabric.

- Silks may be smooth and lightweight or textured and slightly shimmery. Use this material for scarves, jackets, evening purses, and so on.

- Linen has a wonderful, visible texture that enhances crazy quilting, silk ribbon embroidery, and special accessory projects.

- Organza is sheer—perfect for the words of a poem or quotation.

 tip

Pretreated fabrics provide bright images with great contrast—brighter than those printed on home-prepared fabrics.

Home-Treated Fabrics

Unless you purchase a prepared-for-dying (PFD) fabric, any store-bought fabric will have a glaze applied during manufacturing. The glaze keeps the fabric looking fresh and repels dirt. Unfortunately, the glaze also repels inkjet inks, even if the fabric has been soaked in ink fixative first. So, for home-treated fabrics, purchase high-quality, unglazed cottons.

To our knowledge, Bubble Jet Set is the only liquid ink fixative on the market for porous surfaces. It allows you to treat your own fabric at home, but it can be messy and time consuming. As an experiment, we used an entire container of Bubble Jet Set on cotton fabric to see if there was a significant cost savings to treating our own fabric. By the time we washed, dried, and ironed the fabric, soaked it in fixative, allowed it to dry, backed it with freezer paper, and cut it into 8½" × 11" sheets, the cost of pretreated inkjet fabrics seemed like a bargain!

tips

There are times when treating fabric at home is the only choice. Home-treated fabrics are useful when you want to try one of the following applications:

- *Printing on a sheer fabric not available as a commercially pretreated fabric*

- *Printing on a specialty fabric not available as a commercially pretreated fabric*

- *Printing on a print, such as a white-on-cream print*

- *Printing on a tea-dyed fabric for an aged look*

- *Creating a print with a grunge, retro, or vintage effect*

Inkjet Printers

Almost any inkjet printer will print on paper-backed fabrics. Just be aware that the fixative on the fabric is formulated to work with *inkjet printers only*—not laser printers or copy machines.

Load the fabric in the printer just as you would load paper. For an up-and-over printer, place it in the paper tray fabric side down. For a straight-through printer, place it in the paper tray fabric side up.

Refer to the instructions on the pretreated fabric package. Some recommend setting print parameters to plain paper and normal quality, while others recommend other settings. We suggest making test prints at various settings to determine the best setup for your printer and fabric combination.

Some printers exhibit banding (white lines where ink was not applied) when printing on normal-quality print settings. Increasing the quality setting will usually eliminate this. If not, use the printer's utility to clean the printhead. Banding may also occur when an inkjet cartridge has a very low ink level and needs replacing. This is especially noticeable with black ink.

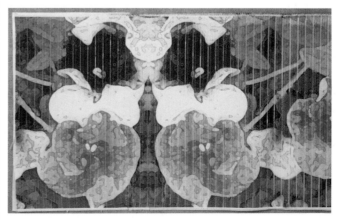

Banding could indicate printer quality that is set too low, a dirty printhead, or a low ink cartridge level.

Some printers have a setting for thick media; others have a lever to flip for thicker media. Choose the card-stock or envelope setting in the printer setup dialog box or flip the lever to allow more room for the media to pass through. This will reduce frustrating jams.

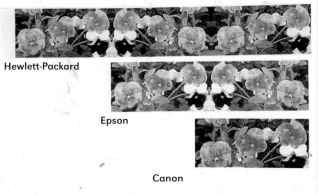

tip

Printers have a maximum length they will print. Even though some software packages claim they can override the manufacturer's limits, it can be a frustrating process. In our opinion, it's much less painful simply to plan the print with the printer's maximum length in mind.

Hewlett-Packard

Epson

Canon

At the time of this writing, the maximum length a Canon Bubblejet printer will print is 33⅓″. An Epson will print 44″ long and an HP (Hewlett-Packard) will print 50″ long.

Inks

In general, there are two kinds of ink: dye-base and pigment-base. Dye-base inks will produce a wider spectrum of colors than pigment-base ink. They are also less expensive, more readily available, and clog

less in the printhead of an inkjet printer. They are water-soluble, however, and less lightfast than pigment-base inks—two serious drawbacks when printing on fabric. The chemical coating on pretreated fabrics addresses the issue of dye-base inks being water-soluble, making them much more water resistant. You can apply a UV spray coating to reduce fading and extend the life of any print. However, we can enthusiastically say that the lightfastness of pigment-base inks is well worth the slightly higher price and the additional fussing they occasionally require.

As a test of lightfastness, we mounted fabric prints on sheets of poster board, covered half of each image with cardboard, and exposed them to direct sunlight. After 30 hours, the dye-base prints showed significant fading, while the pigment-base prints did not. How long will they last? Our tests continue, but after more than 212 hours in direct sunlight, the pigment-base prints still did not show any signs of fading.

Dye-base prints are more sensitive to direct light than pigment-base prints. Fading is evident on the left side of this dye-base print after exposure to sunlight. The right side of the print was covered.

tip

Exposure to direct light is the biggest enemy of an inkjet print on fabric.

Photos & Digital Art

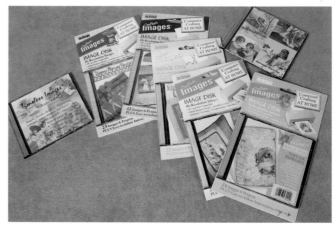

Examples of public-domain or copyright-free images available electronically. Read the copyright notices carefully. Some allow unlimited use, while others allow noncommercial or limited-quantity use.

What can you print, and what constitutes copyright infringement? That is really a difficult question. Neither of us is an attorney and we cannot give legal advice, however, there are resources available to guide you at the U.S. Copyright Office website, www.copyright.gov. We refer to them frequently, because there is no easy answer.

To be absolutely safe, though, print only what you yourself create: your own photos, your own paintings, your own photographs of your own quilts, your own computer drawings, scans of your own artwork, and so on. These are yours to use freely, without question.

Beyond your own artwork, a wide variety of CDs are available with photos and artwork in the public domain (copyrights have expired), copyright-free artwork (such as stock photographs), or artwork that artists offer under a limited-use license. CD collections are available from fabric and craft chain stores, mail-order catalogs, and online stores.

Make sure the format is one you can open with your computer software and that the resolution is high enough to print in the size you want. JPEG is a popular file format that most photo-editing software can recognize, open, and manipulate.

RESOLVING THE RESOLUTION EVOLUTION

Resolution is measured in dots per inch (dpi) or pixels per inch (ppi). For book or magazine reproduction, 300 dpi is considered the resolution of choice. Printing on fabric has more modest resolution requirements. We've found that 150 dpi is suitable for realistic photographs and 72 dpi is sufficient for altered photographs.

When the size of an image is changed, the resolution changes too! Enlarging a photo reduces the resolution (dpi); reducing the size of a photo increases the resolution proportionately. Why? Changing the size of a photo doesn't change the number of pixels; it merely changes the size of the pixels. So, when a photo is enlarged, the pixels are essentially stretched, creating fewer pixels per inch. Conversely, when a photo is reduced in size, the pixels are compressed, fitting more pixels in a square inch. More pixels per square inch = more detail = higher resolution. Fewer pixels per square inch = less detail = lower resolution.

Computers & Scanners

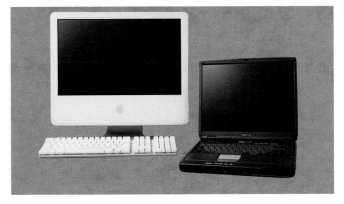

Ours is a dual-platform studio. Lori is devoted to her PC, while Beth is a confirmed Mac user. With the proliferation of software developed for both PC and Mac, both are equally good for working with photos and printing on fabric. Use the platform with which you are most comfortable!

As with most electronics, as the technology ages, the price goes down and the quality, efficiency, and sophistication increases. Excellent-quality flatbed scanners are now available at very low cost.

What can you scan? Just about anything: flat items such as old photos, drawings (think children's artwork), wallpaper borders, handwriting, postcards, greeting cards, postage stamps—or slightly three-dimensional items such as rubber bands, leaves, candy, cookies, nails, body parts, and so on.

Not all scanners will scan items with depth. We found some scanner brands will keep up to ¼" deep in focus, while others will scan only flat planes, such as a flat piece of paper. In our experience, Hewlett-Packard scanners give the best results for thick items.

tip

To prevent light leaks when scanning items with depth, close the lid as much as possible and cover with a piece of dark fabric.

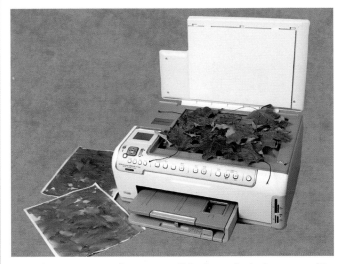

Direct-image scans are best accomplished on a flatbed scanner with some depth of field.

Digital Cameras

It is not necessary to have a high-pixel-rating camera to achieve wonderful photographic images on fabric. The advantage of a higher pixel rating is that images can be printed larger without losing resolution, but a disadvantage is that high-pixel images require more extreme filtering techniques and take longer for filtering (artistic altering) to show.

If we take these same three iris photos below and subject them to two rounds of filtering, we see that the image from the 1-megapixel camera (**A**) reflects the filter changes sooner than the images from the 4-megapixel camera (**B**) and the 7-megapixel camera (**C**).

Notice on page 13 that the detail pulled from image A is beginning to show stair-step edges (called pixelation), while those from images B and C are holding well at a similar size.

Don't worry! The first stitching step is to outline each section in thread. This will effectively smooth ragged lines, making it possible to comfortably enlarge even images taken with a low-pixel-rated camera.

Photos A, B, and C by Beth Wheeler

| Photo **A** was taken with a 1-megapixel digital camera. Printed on photo paper, it would be visually pleasing no larger than 4″ × 6″. | Photo **B** was taken with a 4-megapixel camera and could be printed as an 8″ × 10″ photograph without losing resolution. | Photo **C** was taken with a 7-megapixel camera and could comfortably enlarge to 16″ × 20″. |

All photos on this page by Beth Wheeler

A   B   C

Another thing to consider is that digital cameras often have low-, medium-, and high-resolution exposure settings that allow you to take lower resolution photos than the maximum capacity of the camera. This allows you to take lower resolution photos when you won't need a higher resolution image.

Keep in mind that a high-quality image on a 1-megapixel camera will not be the same size as a high-quality image on a 7-megapixel camera. They will both appear as a 72 dpi image in the computer's software, but the image from the 1-megapixel camera will be much smaller than the image from the 7-megapixel camera. This holds true for all settings (low, medium, and high resolution) on any camera that allows the consumer to adjust the resolution.

tip

The number of exposures on the camera's memory card will decrease as the resolution is increased. Refer to the camera's manual (or the manufacturer's website if you've misplaced the manual) for specific instructions on changing the resolution of the exposures, since each camera is slightly different.

Photo-Editing Software

The variety of software available for photo editing is staggering! Usually a basic photo-editing application is included with scanners and digital cameras. It is adequate for removing red eye, rotating, cropping, and general quality adjustments, but it may not be powerful enough to add artistic touches and abstraction to your images. The good news is: you don't have to spend a fortune to purchase a high-end software package intended for professional graphic designers. You may if you wish, but it's not necessary!

Adobe's Photoshop Elements has many of the tools available in Adobe's Photoshop Creative Suite (CS)— and Elements supports add-on actions, filters, and third-party plug-ins, just as CS does. Actions, filters, and plug-ins are small software applications that work through Photoshop Elements and Photoshop CS. Some are free through the Adobe website (see Sources & Resources, page 77), while some require payment of a modest fee for downloadable functionality. Additionally, many have free trial versions to allow the consumer to sample the features of the software before purchasing.

This book comes with a CD containing a free trial version of Adobe Photoshop Elements 5.0 for PC and all of the instructions and screen capture images in this book are written for 5.0 for PC.

tip

Trial versions usually have limited functionality: they may not allow any altered images to be printed or saved, or they may work only for a limited time. Some manufacturers offer a discount to consumers who download the trial version and then go to the company's website to purchase the full version.

EXAMPLES OF PHOTO-EDITING SOFTWARE

Mac Compatible

- Adobe Photoshop Elements (*highly recommended*)

PC Compatible

- Adobe Photoshop Elements (*highly recommended*)
- Corel Paint Shop Pro
- Microsoft Digital Imaging Suite
- Ulead PhotoImpact
- Kaleidoscope Kreator

tip

Although many software applications are for the PC platform only, do not despair! Those of us who have "Magnificent Macs" can still use the software by installing the cross-platform tool Virtual PC (developed by Connectix and acquired in 2006 by Microsoft). This software makes it possible to run almost any PC-platform software on a Mac.

Be aware, though, that Virtual PC won't run on Intel-based Macs. Mac owners with Intel processors can either use Boot (available from Apple as free download) or a virtualizer such as Parallels or VMWare.

Printing on Fabric FAQs

What kind of inkjet printer do I need to print on fabric?

We've printed on many kinds of printers, including Hewlett-Packard, Canon, Lexmark, Sony, Epson, Kodak, and Dell. Straight-through paper feeds have proved to have fewer jamming problems. We also prefer printers with separate ink cartridges for each color, since we use yellow at nearly twice the rate of any other color.

Do I need special ink to print on fabric?

No, just the ink you normally use in your printer. We prefer the durability of pigment-base ink as opposed to dye-base ink and so we purchase printers for the ink they use. If you are not sure which type of ink your inkjet printer uses, consult the user manual. New printer models and inks are being released constantly.

Can I save money with generic inks?

If you are happy with the quality of the print on paper using generic inks, try it on fabric. Be aware, however, that most printers' warranties are voided if you use ink other than those intended for your printer. These are called OEM (original equipment manufacturer) inks. They are specially formulated to work with the printhead of a specific printer and usually yield the best prints.

Can I refill my inkjet cartridges?

Yes, but be aware that refill inks are not OEM inks and may produce unreliable results. It's easiest to refill cartridges for printers with separate cartridges for each ink color. Those with three colors in the same cartridge are more difficult. If one tank in the cartridge is over-filled, ink can spill into the next tank and cause really funky color reproduction.

Does printing on fabric use a lot of ink?

Printing on fabric uses a little more than printing on paper, but not as much as you might think. Of course, dark backgrounds and heavy coverage with vivid colors will use more ink than images with pastel and light backgrounds.

I printed on the paper side of the inkjet fabric— what do I do now?

No problem—just turn the sheet over and try again. It will go through the printer more than once.

The fabric jams in my printer. What can I do to prevent the jams?

Most fabrics are affected by humidity, but humidity isn't fatal. Try one of these solutions:

- Store fabric flat in the original packaging, which is designed to protect the fabric from humidity, light, and other environmental factors.

- Roll the fabric with the paper side out and hold for a few seconds.

- Warm the fabric with an iron. We suggest warming the paper side, just in case there's something on the face of the iron that could spot the fabric. Weight the fabric with a heavy book until it cools.

- Set the printer for envelope, cardstock, or T-shirt transfer to allow thicker media to travel through the paper path.

- Use the straight-through manual slot rather than the up-and-over paper path.

- Apply a strip of masking tape to the leading edge on the paper side. This will help the paper feed through more smoothly.

- Trim a tiny triangle ($1/4$" or so) from the corner that jams.

preparing
& altering
photographs

Our APPROACH TO USING THE COMPUTER AS A
DESIGN TOOL INCREASES THE RANGE OF PHOTOGRAPHS
THAT CAN BE USED. POOR COLOR BALANCE, SKEWED PERSPECTIVE,
SOFT FOCUS, AND QUESTIONABLE COMPOSITION CAN ALL BE
CORRECTED OR BYPASSED, AND EVEN MARGINAL PHOTOGRAPHS
CAN BE TURNED INTO EYE-CATCHING STITCHED PIECES.

Composing a Photo

The closer the better! Get as close to the subject as possible, removing extraneous background material that can be distracting. The larger the scope of the composition, the more items there are to be outlined and the more the focus is spread out, so move in to control the focus and drama.

Isolating one design element increases the graphic impact of the composition. In the original photo below, an individual rose gets lost in the crowd, while in the center photo, the rose is in the spotlight. To increase the abstraction of the piece, zoom in even more, concentrating on shadows and motion.

Just how close you can get is determined by the zoom or macro capabilities of your camera. Check the manual to determine how close you can get to the subject and still keep it in focus and whether there is a macro feature to facilitate closer work.

tips

- *Isolate the subject by getting close enough to eliminate confusing backgrounds. A good rule of thumb is to sit at the computer with your eyes closed, then open them and glance at the image on the computer monitor. Your eyes should go directly to the subject, not to something in the background.*

- *When a good photo opportunity presents itself, shoot the subject from different angles and at varying distances. This allows artistic flexibility later, when the creative muse may sing a different song.*

- *For the sharpest image, set the digital camera for high-resolution exposure. The file will be large and the memory card will hold fewer images, but the quality will be higher.*

- *We suggest using a tripod to reduce any extraneous movement and produce the sharpest image possible.*

Original photo

Spotlight a single flower.

Tighten the focus even more.

All photos on this page by Beth Wheeler

Scanning a Photo

Scanning, which involves just a few simple steps, allows the artist to transform any photo into a digital file, ready for altering.

1. Before scanning, take a moment to consider how you will use the digital image. If it will ultimately be used as a large piece and require a lot of enlargement, scan the photo at a higher resolution. The target is about 150 dpi in the final enlargement (to print on fabric).

2. Clean the glass of the scanner bed.

3. Place the item to be scanned on the glass and close the lid.

4. If the item is thick and prevents the scanner lid from closing completely, cover the top and sides with a piece of dark fabric to prevent light leaks.

5. Set the scanner software to color, even if the original is a black-and-white photo. This creates an image with greater depth and detail.

6. Set the scanner software to the desired resolution. The higher the setting, the longer it will take to scan and the larger the file will be.

7. Preview the scan (if that feature is available on your scanner) and tighten the selection box so only the desired image is being scanned.

8. Once the scanner has worked its magic, save the file in TIFF format, not JPEG. JPEG uses a compression algorithm, effectively eliminating some original information from the photo. A TIFF file is larger than a JPEG, but all the information about the original image is retained.

Repairing a Photo

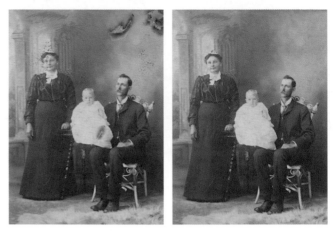

Whether you are working with a vintage black-and-white photo with spots, wrinkles, and tears, a decades-old four-color print with color shifts, or a brand-new digital photo, all have imperfections that can be corrected with Adobe Photoshop Elements, Adobe Photoshop CS, or other photo-editing software.

AUTOMATIC REPAIR FEATURES

Adobe Photoshop Elements has powerful automatic repair features that are a great starting point for repairing old and damaged photos.

1. Select the **Quick Fix** tab.

2. Apply **Auto Smart Fix**.

3. Apply **Auto Levels**.

4. Apply **Auto Contrast**.

5. Apply **Auto Color Correction**.

6. If you like the repair, save it. If you don't, use the **Undo** command in the **Edit** drop-down menu to undo the most recent action.

ADDITIONAL REPAIR FEATURES

Spots, wrinkles, and tears may be smoothed away with a few simple steps.

1. Select the **Full Edit** tab.

2. Select the **clone stamp** tool (it looks like a rubber stamp).

3. Adjust the **brush size** as desired.

4. Choose an *undamaged* area of similar color and texture by holding down the **Alt** key and clicking with your mouse.

5. Move the cursor back to the *blemished* area, then **click and drag** (or simply click) to replace damaged pixels with copies of the new pixels. Repeat along a linear wrinkle, fold, or tear until you are happy with the image.

6. Select **File: Save As** to save the image as a separate file from the original. You never know when a creative moment will occur and you'll want to try something different.

Altering a Photo

Adobe Photoshop Elements and Adobe Photoshop CS each have built-in filters to alter and enhance digital images. Experiment with the filters to find which effects you like the best. We've logged hundreds of hours developing combinations of filters that work best with our photo styles. The following are a few simple techniques with maximum visual impact that work well when artwork is enlarged and quilted. In a later chapter, we will learn how to prepare these altered photos for printing on fabric.

PENCIL-SKETCH PORTRAITS

Turn a simple snapshot into a striking pencil-sketch portrait with a simple Adobe Photoshop plug-in. Anyone would be delighted with this for a housewarming, new-baby, wedding, graduation, Mother's Day, or anniversary gift!

Choosing the Photo and Software

Although no one could resist those chubby cheeks and impish smile, this is not a professional-looking portrait. It would be perfect in a scrapbook but needs work before it is ready for printing on fine fabric and mounting in a quality frame.

For our software, we chose **Sketch Master from Redfield**, a downloadable PC plug-in for Adobe Photoshop Elements/Photoshop CS (see Sources & Resources, page 77). The download includes simple instructions for loading the plug-in.

Preparing the Photo

1. **Open** the photo in Adobe Photoshop Elements.

2. **Repair** any blemishes (see Repairing a Photo, page 18).

3. Apply the Unsharp Mask filter by selecting **Enhance: Unsharp Mask**. Drag the slider bars for the amount, radius, and threshold. This sharpens the image by increasing the contrast of each pixel's outline (for Adobe Photoshop CS, select Filter: Sharpen: Unsharp Mask).

Altering the Photo Using Sketch Master

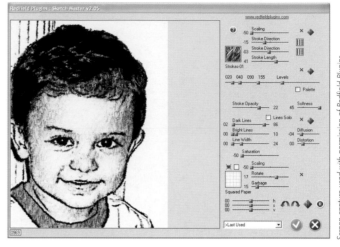

Sketch Master allows you to choose from a variety of background textures and stroke patterns.

1. Select the **Lead Pencil** mode.

2. First try the **random generator**, which will select random combinations of features for you, allowing a quick view of various effects with one click. Try several variations to see which one you like.

3. If you wish, play with the **slider bars** in the Sketch Master control panel to adjust the various features individually.

4. Select **File: Save As** to save the image as a separate file from the original.

SEPIA TONING

Photo by Beth Wheeler

Give a four-color photo instant drama with sepia tones. Many photo-editing applications have an automatic sepia-tone filter, but here is another way to add the effect and maintain control over saturation, contrast, and lightness/darkness.

Preparing the Photo for Sepia Tone

1. **Open** the photo in Adobe Photoshop Elements.

2. **Repair** any blemishes (see Repairing a Photo, page 18).

3. Apply the Unsharp Mask filter by selecting **Enhance: Unsharp Mask**. Drag the slider bars for the amount, radius, and threshold. This sharpens the image by increasing the contrast of each pixel's outline.

Adding Sepia-Tone Color

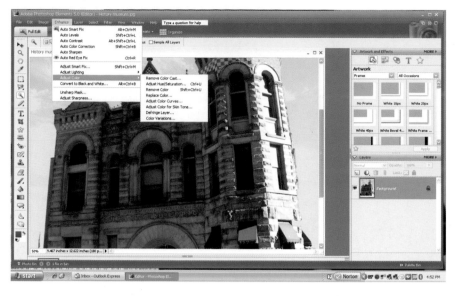

1. Select **Enhance: Adjust Color: Remove Color** to change the image from color to black and white.

2. Select **Enhance: Adjust Color: Color Variations**.

3. Select the **Midtones** button. Click the **Increase the red** button and the **Decrease the blue** button to create soft brown (sepia) tones.

4. Select **Filter: Noise: Add Noise** to age the image. Drag the slider bar until you are pleased with the effect, then click **OK**.

Fine-Tuning the Image

3. As a final tweak, if the photo is of a place or thing (anything other than a person), we almost always increase the contrast. Select **Enhance: Adjust Lighting: Brightness/Contrast**.

4. If you don't like the effect once it's applied, simply use the **Undo** command to remove the contrast adjustment.

5. When you are pleased with the image, select **File: Save As** to save the image as a separate file from the original.

1. Apply **Image: Mode: RGB** color. This moves the image back to color mode, where Adobe Photoshop Elements' powerful adjustment tools can be applied.

2. Select **Image: Adjustments: Hue/Saturation**. Slide the saturation slider bar in both directions to see how it affects the image. Play with it until you are pleased with the color.

KALEIDOSCOPIC IMAGERY

There are a number of plug-ins for Adobe Photoshop Elements and Adobe Photoshop CS that create kaleidoscopic effects. **Kaleidoscope Kreator from Kaleidoscope Collections** is (in our opinion) hands down the easiest software to use with the highest-resolution results (see Sources & Resources, page 77).

Preparing the Photo

Photo by Beth Wheeler

1. **Open** the photo in Adobe Photoshop Elements. For best results, zoom in on and select one design element from the photo.

2. **Repair** any blemishes (see Repairing a Photo, page 18).

3. Apply the Unsharp Mask filter by selecting **Enhance: Unsharp Mask**. Drag the slider bars for the amount, radius, and threshold. This sharpens the image by increasing the contrast of each pixel's outline (for Adobe Photoshop CS, select Filter: Sharpen: Unsharp Mask).

4. Increase the contrast. Select **Enhance: Adjust Lighting: Brightness/Contrast** (for Adobe Photoshop CS, select Image: Adjustments: Brightness/Contrast).

5. Select **File: Save As** to save the image as a separate file from the original.

Creating a Kaleidoscopic Composition

1. **Open** the photo in Kaleidoscope Kreator.

2. Select **Edit: Shape** to choose a kaleidoscope template from the 56 templates available.

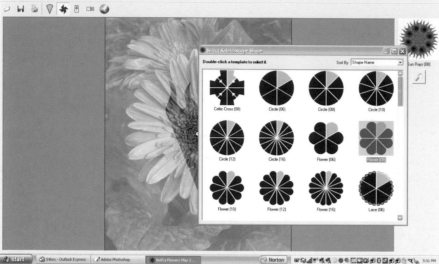

3. A navigation box displays the position of the template on the photo. **Move the photo under the template**, or resize and rotate the photo to create a kaleidoscopic composition. A preview of the result is shown in the upper right corner of the screen.

4. **Save** several different kaleidoscopic images as high-quality JPEG or TIFF files. This will allow you to open your favorite image in Adobe Photoshop Elements later to resize, divide, print, and quilt.

Hundreds of kaleidoscopic variations are possible. Have fun and experiment!

Photo by Lori Marquette

12-point Sunburst template

Pinwheel template

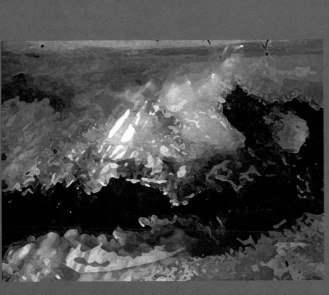

6-petal Lotus template

Celtic Cross template

FUNKY COLORIZING

Altering the original colors of a photo can make a so-so image *fabulous*! Experimenting with different color effects on the same image is a great way to see the powerful range of this technique. Watch how a different funky color can change the whole mood of a photo.

Preparing the Photo

1. **Open** the photo in Adobe Photoshop Elements.

2. **Repair** any blemishes (see Repairing a Photo, page 18).

3. Apply the Unsharp Mask filter by selecting **Enhance: Unsharp Mask**. Drag the slider bars for the amount, radius, and threshold. This sharpens the image by increasing the contrast of each pixel's outline (for Adobe Photoshop CS, select Filter: Sharpen: Unsharp Mask).

4. Increase the contrast. Select **Enhance: Adjust Lighting: Brightness/Contrast** (for Adobe Photoshop CS, select Image: Adjustments: Brightness/Contrast).

5. **Apply artistic filters** until you are pleased with the image.

Adjusting the Color

1. Select **Enhance: Adjust Color: Adjust Hue/Saturation** (for Adobe Photoshop CS, select Image: Adjustments: Hue/Saturation).

2. In the **Edit** box, select **Master** to adjust all colors simultaneously, or select a specific color from the drop-down menu to adjust that color only.

3. Slide the **hue slider bar** to the left or right to change the color. It doesn't take much adjustment of the slider bar to create dramatic changes, but try the bar at the extreme left and extreme right to see just how far the effect can be pushed.

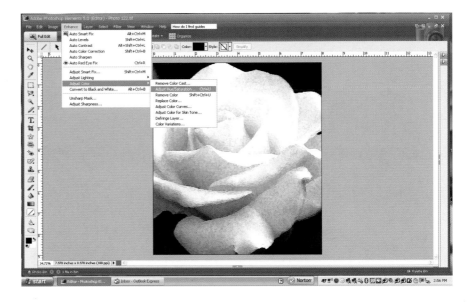

4. Experiment with the **saturation slider bar**, too. *Remember: any change can be reversed with the **Undo** command.*

5. Try clicking the **Colorize** box for some interesting monochromatic effects.

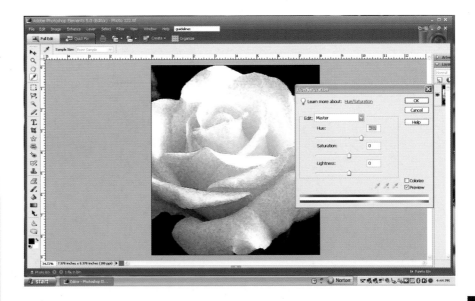

6. When you are pleased with the results, select **File: Save As.** Save several versions of the image as separate files from the original, as below.

ADDING TEXT

In Loving Memory of Alice Ferrell
by her niece Beth Johnson Wheeler

Her struggle with Alzheimer's Disease
did not diminish her beautiful spirit.

9/12/2006

There are two common ways to add words to a photographic composition—both are easy and give great results. Adding words is a great way to personalize a piece, especially if your work is ultimately intended as a gift to someone special.

Adding Words Directly on the Image

1. **Open** the photo in Adobe Photoshop Elements.

2. **Repair** any blemishes (see Repairing a Photo, page 18).

3. Apply the Unsharp Mask filter by selecting **Enhance: Unsharp Mask**. Drag the slider bars for the amount, radius, and threshold. This sharpens the image by increasing the contrast of each pixel's outline (for Adobe Photoshop CS, select Filter: Sharpen: Unsharp Mask).

4. Increase the contrast. Select **Enhance: Adjust Lighting: Brightness/Contrast** (for Adobe Photoshop CS, select Image: Adjustments: Brightness/Contrast).

5. **Apply artistic filters** until you are pleased with the image.

6. Select **File: Save As** to save as a separate file from the original.

7. Choose the **Text Tool** (it looks like a capital letter T) from the toolbox and position the tool on the photograph. Type the desired words in the text box.

8. Choose the **font, size, style,** and **color of type**.

9. **Deselect** the text box by clicking off it.

10. Adobe Photoshop Elements automatically adds a layer just for the type. Until the layers are merged, the type may be changed or moved.

Adding Words Separately

Words created in any word-processing application may be printed on fabric and appliquéd onto or pieced into a quilt. Simply key the words in the document window, add any effects you wish, and print on fabric.

This might be a good place to use a sheer inkjet fabric to create an ethereal effect.

COLOR SPOTLIGHTING

Spotlighting creates a powerful visual image by drawing the focus to a particular area of the photo. The contrast between the spotlighted area and the background adds considerable drama to any image. You can spotlight any area of a photo that you desire, from the smallest detail to entire sections. As always, you should explore the full potential of the technique by applying it to different types of images. Here we've chosen a flower, but this technique can be applied to people, buildings, or even totally abstract images.

Preparing the Photo

Photo by Lori Marquette

1. **Open** the photo in Adobe Photoshop Elements.

2. **Repair** any blemishes (See Repairing a Photo, page 18).

3. Apply the Unsharp Mask filter by selecting **Enhance: Unsharp Mask**. Drag the slider bars for the amount, radius, and threshold. This sharpens the image by increasing the contrast of each pixel's outline (for Adobe Photoshop CS, select Filter: Sharpen: Unsharp Mask).

Selecting & Removing the Color

1. Use the **Magic Wand, Magnetic Lasso,** or another selection tool to define the area to remain colored.

2. Choose **Select: Inverse** to choose everything except the area to remain colored.

3. Select **Enhance: Adjust Color: Remove Color** to remove the color from all the selected areas and leave the color in the area originally defined by the selection tool (for Adobe Photoshop CS, select Image: Adjustments: Desaturate).

Fine-Tuning the Image

Now is the time to make desired **adjustments in color** (hue/saturation) or **contrast** (brightness/contrast).

When you are pleased with the image, select **File: Save As** to save the image as a separate file from the original.

printing photos
on fabric

READY TO PRINT ON FABRIC? HAS THE PHOTO
BEEN REPAIRED AND UNSHARP MASK APPLIED? HAS IT BEEN ALTERED
AND ADJUSTED FOR ANY DESIRED SPECIAL EFFECTS? YOU ARE NOW
READY TO MAKE A TEST PRINT.

Making a Test Print

At this point, resize the image to 8″ × 10″ (if necessary) and make a test print on paper. If you like it and are ready to move on and print on fabric, increase the contrast +25%. The resulting image may look garish on the monitor, but you'll be pleased with the print on fabric. We call this the Rule of 25. It has served us well and has been helpful to countless students in our classes over the years.

 *tip:* Rule of 25

When you like the print on paper, increase the contrast +25% before printing on fabric.

Making an 8″ × 10″ Print

1. Insert the pretreated fabric in the paper tray of the printer.

2. Set the printer preferences for cardstock or heavyweight paper.

3. Set the quality for plain paper or matte-finish photo paper.

4. Print.

5. Allow the ink to dry thoroughly (at least an hour for dye-base ink; 24 hours for pigment-base ink).

6. Remove the backing.

7. Rinse, if recommended by the fabric manufacturer. Dry completely.

 *tip:* Separating Fabric and Backing

Scrape the corner gently with your thumbnail. The backing and fabric should separate easily. If they don't, try heating the backing side with a dry iron to loosen the bond between the layers. This works for fabric sheets with laminated backing. Check the manufacturer's instructions; if the backing has been applied with an adhesive, you should not apply heat to it.

Making a Small Print:
Reducing the Image Size

Want to print your image smaller than the original image size?
No problem. Follow the steps below to reduce the image size
to fit your specific needs.

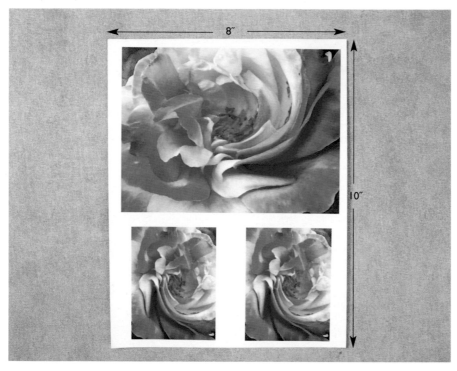

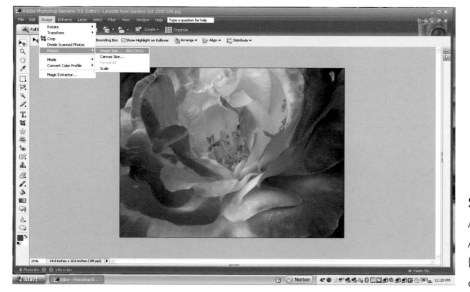

1. Select **Image: Resize: Image Size** from the pull-down menu in Adobe Photoshop Elements (for Adobe Photoshop CS, select Image: Image Size; a dialog box will appear offering several choices).

ALTERED PHOTO ARTISTRY

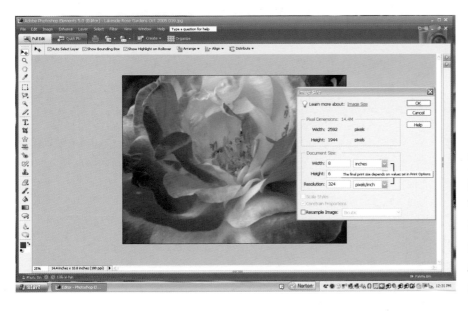

2. With the **Resample Image** box unchecked, resize the image. You'll notice that the width and height will change, as well as the numbers in the **Resolution** box. As you reduce the image size, the resolution will increase.

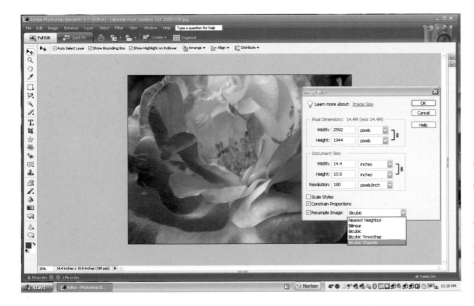

3. With the **Resample Image: Constrain Proportions** box checked and the **Bicubic Sharper** selected, resize the width. You'll notice that the number in the height box will change automatically. This is good for preventing distortion of the image's proportions.

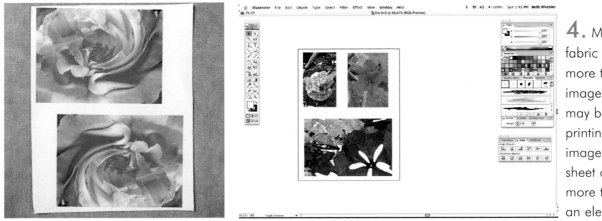

Example of a sheet run through the printer twice, printing the image at each end of the sheet

Electronic layout with more than one small photo

4. Make the most of a fabric sheet by printing more than one small image on a sheet. This may be accomplished by printing an individual image on each end of a sheet or by arranging more than one photo on an electronic layout page.

Making a Large Print

AUTOMATICALLY TILED PRINT

Want your print larger than 8½" × 11", but the printer is only 8½" wide? No problem! By tiling or printing it as a poster image, you can enlarge the image considerably. How much depends on the quality of the original image.

Many printers offer automatic tiling or poster printing as an option in the printer setup box. Check the printer manual or look for Layout Options in the print dialog box.

Using the printer to tile an image automatically enlarges the original image and divides it into the number of segments chosen. For instance, 2 × 2 tiling prints an image over 4 sheets: 2 sheets across and 2 sheets down. Some programs can perform up to 4 × 4 tiling, dividing the image across 16 separate sheets for assembly later.

1

2

3

4

2 × 2 tiling (two sheets across and two sheets down, for a total of four sheets)

If your printer does not support automatic tiling, or if you are working with a Macintosh operating on OS X, see Making a Large Print: Manually Tiled Print below.

MANUALLY TILED PRINT

Adobe Photoshop Elements and Adobe Photoshop CS make it easy to enlarge and divide an image manually.

1. Enlarge the image to the desired size. The width should be in multiples of 8″, and the length should be in multiples of 10½″. If the image is not in these proportions, some cropping will occur.

2. Enlarge the original image 10% at a time with the **Bicubic Smoother** selected. It takes a few minutes longer to enlarge this way, but the resolution degrades less than if the enlargement were made in one step.

3. Activate the ruler so you can see the image dimensions. Select **View: Show ruler.**

4. Pull a guideline from the left-hand edge to the 8″, 16″, and 24″ marks (every 8″).

5. Pull a guideline from the top to the 10½″, 21″, and 31½″ marks (every 10½″).

6. With the selection tool, select and copy one 8″ × 10½″ segment.

7. Paste the segment into a new document.

8. Save it as a segment number, such as iris seg-1, iris seg-2, iris seg-3, and so on.

9. Repeat with the remaining segments.

10. Print each segment on a sheet of fabric.

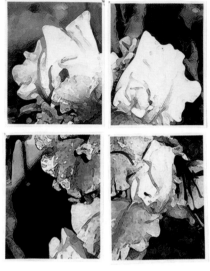

11. Mark the segment number on each segment, always in the same corner, as it emerges from the printer. Use a fade-out pen if you are concerned about numbers being visible after the panel is assembled.

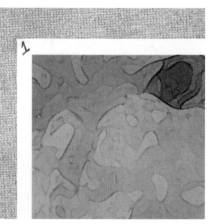

12. Allow the ink to dry thoroughly. Remove the backing from each segment. (Do not rinse the segment sheets at this time. We'll rinse later, if necessary.)

Assembling a Tiled Print

3. Pin them together along the edge of the printed image (not necessarily an even ¼″ seam allowance).

4. Stitch along the line with neutral or monofilament thread in the machine top and bobbin.

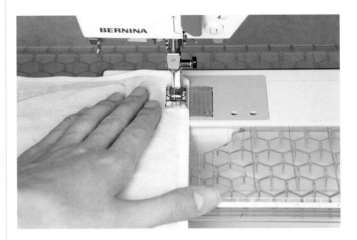

5. Press the seam allowances open. Check for white gaps on the print side. If white gaps are visible, stitch the seam slightly deeper.

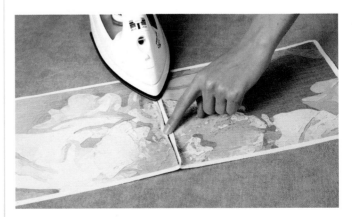

1. Arrange the segments in order on a work surface.

2. Place segments 1 and 2 together, right sides facing.

6. Repeat Steps 1–5 for the segments of each column.

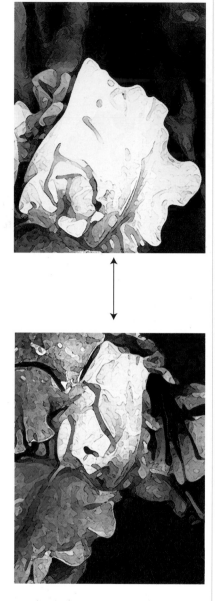

7. Join the columns into a single panel. Press well.

8. Rinse the panel if recommended by the manufacturer and if dye-base ink has been used for the print. Dry completely.

sewing equipment & supplies

OUR TECHNIQUE GIVES THE ARTIST AN OPPORTUNITY TO USE THREAD AS AN INTEGRAL ARTISTIC TOOL TO ADD TEXTURE, DIMENSION, AND DEFINITION TO THE IMAGES PRINTED ON FABRIC. THE PROCESS IS RELATIVELY SIMPLE, BUT THE RESULTS ARE STUNNING, AND FINISHED PIECES ARE EASILY RECOGNIZED AS THE FINE ART THEY ARE.

Stabilizer/Batting

Synthetic fleece (thick dense quilt batting; not sweatshirt fleece) is an excellent batting for this technique. The dense matting of synthetic strands stabilizes the fibers of the print during stitching and protects the print from stress when hanging—framed or unframed. Since our pieces are not intended as bed or lap quilts, snuggle-ability is not a concern.

Fleece is available in lightweight, medium-weight, and heavyweight and can come with fusible adhesive on one side, both sides, or neither. We prefer medium-weight fusible fleece for small pieces (8″ × 10″ to 16″ × 21″) and thicker fleece for larger pieces. The projects in this book assume you are using fusible fleece.

If you can't find fusible fleece, consider using a spray-on fusible, such as 606 Spray and Fix from Oklahoma Embroidery Supply & Design (OESD), or temporary quilt-basting spray.

adding thread details

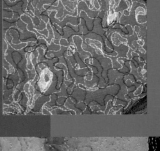

AFTER YOU'VE CHOSEN AN IMAGE, ALTERED AND MANIPULATED IT WITH PHOTO-EDITING SOFTWARE, AND PRINTED IT ON FABRIC, THE NEXT STEP IS TO ADD SOME COLOR AND TEXTURE WITH THREAD. THIS PROCESS OF ADDING THREAD DETAILS REALLY GOES BEYOND MERE EMBELLISHMENT OR ENHANCEMENT; IT IS YOUR OPPORTUNITY TO "PAINT" THE IMAGE WITH THREAD AND ADD DRAMATIC DETAIL THAT MAKES YOUR WORK STAND OUT.

Preparing for Stitching

1. Cut a piece of fusible fleece slightly larger than the printed panel.

2. If the piece will be framed or worked into a constructed piece, such as a jacket, no fabric backing is needed; if the piece will be bound, as a wall quilt, for example, cut a piece of backing the same size as the fleece.

3. Bond the fleece to the wrong side of the printed panel with an iron, following the manufacturer's directions. Work from the center to the outer edges of the panel to prevent unwanted bubbles.

4. If you are using backing, fuse or baste the backing in place.

Making an Outline Map

When the panel sandwich (fleece and printed top) is under the sewing machine's needle, it can be very difficult to tell where you are on the panel, especially if the piece has been rotated. In addition, the altering of the photo before printing complicates the process. We have devised an outline map to help during outline stitching.

To make an outline map, use the **test print** of the completed image on paper. Use a medium-point felt marker in a dark color (black or dark blue) to indicate where you will stitch each section outline.

Draw your outline map on the test print. The outline map will act as a guide when you add thread details.

tip

If it is difficult to identify image details in a print of the completed image, try examining a print of the original photo, before any alteration was performed.

Outline Stitching

The outline stitching is a very important part of the composition. It adds critical definition to the abstract image, as well as creating motion and setting the style for the stitching.

In our studio, we outline almost exclusively with black upholstery thread. Occasionally a dark blue, gray, or brown will be used, but black is by far the most common color of choice. It provides a good contrast with the print, which is very important when the quilt is viewed from a distance.

Even using a heavy thread for the outline isn't enough to define detail adequately, so we stitch around design elements three times to increase the definition. The three rounds should not be stitched exactly on top of one another; offsetting the lines slightly adds texture, motion, and style to the outline. For instance, smooth sketchy lines in gentle undulations create a very different style effect than lines with corners and points.

1. Fit the sewing machine with a darning or free-motion foot.

2. Insert a size 16 needle.

3. Thread the machine top with upholstery thread (black, brown, navy, or other dark color).

4. Use a bobbin with monofilament thread.

5. Drop the machine's feed dogs.

6. Set the machine for a straight stitch, 10–12 stitches per inch.

7. Referring to the outline map, begin working on a section close to the center.

8. Outline the section 3 times, offsetting rounds of stitching lines slightly to increase the interest and texture.

9. Repeat around each section or design element in the piece, working from the center to the outer edges. Use the outline map as a guide, referring to it as you outline stitch the piece.

Notice how the outline stitching defines the folds of this flower, adds dramatic effect to the image, and acts as a "border" between sections of fill-stitching.

tip: Outlining Is Easy!

You almost can't make a mistake with our method. The idea is to outline each section with three wiggly lines of free-motion stitching. This hides any imperfections on the edges of the photo and is very forgiving. If necessary, you can stitch over an area once or twice until you've evened out any big bumps or stray wiggles. Relax and enjoy the process!

Outline stitching

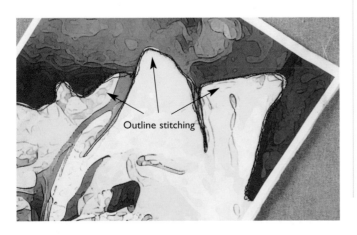

Filling in with Texture

Castle Gallery,
20″ × 16″, 2006
by Beth Wheeler
and Lori Marquette.

Photo by Lori Marquette

All surface stitching on our work has been done in free-motion straight stitches. To create the texture of water, wind, clouds, grass, brick, stone, and so on with no color, use monofilament thread in the machine top and bobbin. We routinely use monofilament in the bobbin to prevent any color showing on the top and to reduce the number of times the bobbin must be changed.

One piece may require eight to ten different top threads; the thought of eight to ten bobbin changes in one piece is likely to cause nightmares. Using monofilament thread in the bobbin means stopping to change the bobbin only when it runs out of thread—or about once an hour during frenzied stitching.

Control the contrast and texture with the concentration and shape of your stitch patterns. Subtle but effective contrast is achieved by switching between heavy and light coverage of straight stitches. Experiment with various stitch shapes, patterns, and scales to achieve different textural effects.

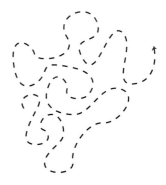

Meander quilting with no points

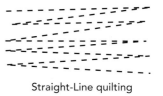

Straight-Line quilting

Echo quilting

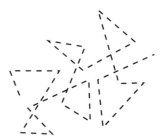

Meander quilting with points

Filling in with Color

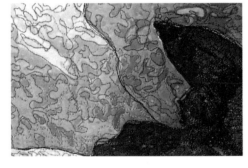

Balance,
16˝ × 21˝, 2006
by Beth Wheeler.

tip: Stitching Time

How long does it take to add thread embellishment to an assembled panel? This is a question we hear often. After working hundreds of compositions, we can estimate the following, calculated on our usual stitch speed (55 mph) and coverage (moderate):

■ *Each 8˝ × 10˝ print takes about 20–30 minutes to stitch.*

■ *Larger panels (more than 9 prints stitched together) take longer, because of fatigue after several hours of stitching.*

Solid-color cotton, silk, and rayon threads, Mylar tapes, metallic-wrapped or metallic-twist threads, and variegated threads each have a place in thread enhancement. Stitches done in cotton threads have a matte finish, while rayon and silk have sheen. Mylar holographic tapes give stitches a sharp sparkle, while metallic-wrapped or metallic-twist threads have a more subtle shine. Variegated threads can be blends of monochromatic, contrasting, or coordinating colors and tones.

Working with large areas of white was a particular challenge until we began combining stitches done in white rayon thread with stitches done in white iridescent Mylar. The sparkle added depth and excitement in a space that could have been boring.

Finishing

Will your piece be framed, gallery wrapped, bound as a wall quilt, or worked into another composition, such as a pillow, a tote bag, a mantel scarf, wearable art, or some other project? There are many ways to incorporate art quilts into individual lifestyles!

FRAMING & GALLERY WRAPPING

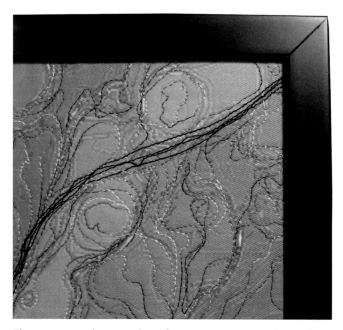

There are two basic styles of mounting on wood stretcher bars for hanging on a wall: classic framing and gallery wrapping. Gallery wrapping is the preliminary step to classic framing, permitting a change in plans at a later date.

Gallery wrapping involves mounting the stitched piece on stretcher frames. To maximize the printed image, we add 3″-wide strips of fabric around all four sides. This frames the image tastefully and allows the borderlike fabric to provide stability when it is wrapped around wooden bars and secured. Gallery wraps are popular in the fine-art industry now, helping raise art quilts to the fine-art arena.

 tip

Gallery-wrapped pieces may be hung as is or mounted in a classic frame. It's easy to change your mind and add a classic frame later, since gallery wrapping is the first step in the process of classic framing.

FINISHING AS A WALLHANGING

If you planned ahead and added thread embellishment to a three-layer quilt sandwich for use as a wallhanging, it's a simple matter to finish the piece. Bind or face the edges and add a rod pocket, using a favorite method, or finish with a satin-stitch edging.

Satin-Stitch Edging

1. Trim the edges with a rotary cutter and ruler on a self-healing mat for a clean edge.

2. Stitch ⅛" away from the raw edges with a straight stitch in rayon thread in the machine top and in the bobbin.

3. Work a short, wide (1mm long and 3mm wide) zigzag stitch around the edges, with the zig portion of the stitch on the quilt's edge and the zag just barely off the edge. Work one edge at a time, leaving thread tails to help begin stitching on the next round.

tip

Sometimes when beginning an overlapping round of stitching, the machine does not feed properly. Pull gently on the thread tail from the previous round to coax the piece forward and to prevent a lump of thread from forming at the lead edge.

4. Set the machine for a shorter, wider zigzag stitch. This second round of stitching fills in any thread gaps for a densely stitched edge.

5. Trim the tails and secure the cut ends with seam sealant.

If you changed your mind along the way and now need to add a backing, this is the time to do so. Position the wrong side of the backing fabric against the wrong side of the stitched piece, and baste or pin in place. Stitch through all the layers to secure; finish the raw edges as desired.

projects

𝒰SE THIS SUMMARY AS A QUICK REFERENCE TO THE BASIC STEPS INVOLVED IN PREPARING YOUR PHOTO, PRINTING IT ON FABRIC, AND EMBELLISHING IT WITH THREAD. THEN INCORPORATE YOUR WORK INTO ONE OF THE PROJECTS BELOW.

BASIC STEPS SUMMARY

1. Choose or scan your photo. Crop, resize, and repair blemishes as necessary.

2. Add artistic filtering to achieve the desired look. Apply the Unsharp Mask filter and save the revised photo as a new file.

3. Make a test print on paper to use as the outline map.

4. Increase the contrast +25% and print the image on pretreated fabric. Allow the ink to dry thoroughly.

5. Remove the backing. Assemble tiled prints into a panel, if necessary.

6. Rinse, if recommended by the fabric manufacturer. Dry completely.

7. Layer with fusible fleece and (optional) fabric backing.

8. Outline stitch each section with dark thread.

9. Fill stitch sections with texture and/or color.

Book Covers

Photo by Lori Marquette

Fits a 6″ × 9″ × 1¼″ book.

Give someone special the opportunity to showcase a vintage family photo, picture-perfect garden, or other memento. For your convenience, the project instructions have been written without the use of the piping shown in this photo.

MATERIALS

- Photograph (vertical)
- 1 sheet pretreated inkjet fabric
- ½ yard fabric for outside of cover
- ½ yard lining fabric
- ¼ yard fusible fleece
- All-purpose sewing thread
- Hand-sewing supplies
- 24″ zipper
- 9 inches 1″-wide belt webbing for handle

CUTTING

From the cover fabric, cut:

- 1 back, 7″ × 10″
- 2 sides, 2½″ × 24″
- 1 gusset, 2¼″ × 8″

From the lining, cut:

- 1 front, 7″ × 10″
- 1 back, 7″ × 10″
- 2 sides, 2½″ × 24″
- 1 gusset, 2¼″ × 8″
- 2 pockets, 6″ × 10″

From the fusible fleece, cut:

- 2 pieces, 7″ × 10″

tip

Use a ¼″ seam allowance throughout.

Stitching with a serger is not necessary for the successful completion of this project, but it does create a sturdy seam with finished edges. You may overcast the seam allowances instead, if desired.

INSTRUCTIONS

1. Choose a vertical photo that will size well to 7″ × 10″.

2. Follow Steps 1–9 in the Basic Steps Summary (page 54). For Step 3, make a 7″ × 10″ test print for the outline map. In Step 7, do not use a backing.

3. After you have fill-stitched the printed image with texture and color, press it well, trim it to 7″ × 10″, and set it aside.

4. Fold over ¼″ on one long edge of each pocket piece and press. Fold over another ¼″ and straight stitch along the edge, close to the first fold.

5. Fuse fleece to the wrong side of the back cover piece.

6. Lay the stitched front panel and back cover piece fleece side up, with the front on the left and the back on the right. Add the lining pieces, then the pockets on top, right side up. Position the pockets so the raw edges are even on 3 sides and the hemmed edge is toward the center. Baste around each panel to hold the layers in place. Round the corners slightly.

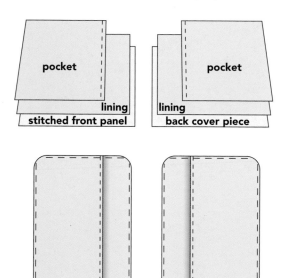

7. Fold the cover side piece in half lengthwise, wrong sides together, and press. Repeat with the second cover side piece and with both lining side pieces to make 4 zipper casings 1½″ x 24″.

8. With the *closed* zipper right side up, position a cover zipper casing on each side, with the folded edges next to the zipper teeth. Baste in place. Turn the zipper over and repeat to baste the lining zipper casings in place. Using a zipper foot, topstitch close to the zipper teeth, and remove the basting stitches. Trim the finished zipper assembly to 2¼″ wide.

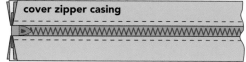

9. Place the cover gusset right side up. Center the raw ends of the webbing on each short end of the cover gusset. Stitch across the ends to secure the webbing.

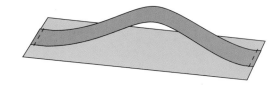

tip: Even Easier Instructions
Want a quick gift? Appliqué a stitched photo print onto a presewn book cover.

10. Layer the following pieces, aligned along one short edge: cover gusset (with webbing) right side up, zipper assembly right side down, lining gusset right side down. Stitch across the short end through all the layers. Do the same with the other short end and stitch through all the layers to form a loop. (Stitch the short ends only, not the long edges.) Turn the loop right side out.

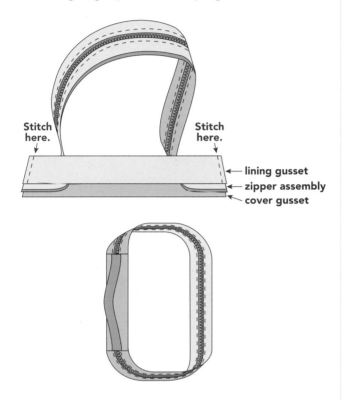

Stitch here.

Stitch here.

← lining gusset
← zipper assembly
← cover gusset

11. *Open the zipper all the way.* Pin the gusset/zipper loop to the front piece, with right sides together and raw edges even. Center the gusset on the left side of the front piece, so (with the zipper open) the zipper pull is near the bottom left corner of the panel. Stitch around with a serger; or use a straight stitch, then finish the raw edges with a zig-zag stitch.

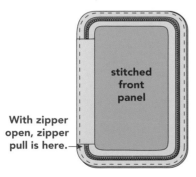

stitched front panel

With zipper open, zipper pull is here. →

12. Pin the gusset/zipper loop to the back lining piece, with right sides together and raw edges even. *Check the zipper; it should be open!* Stitch around as for the front.

13. Turn the piece right side out through the open zipper.

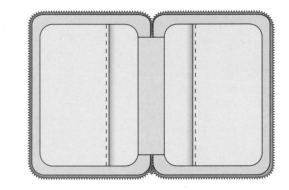

tip: Create a Cover for Any Book!

Measure the book's length, width, and thickness. Add 1˝ to these measurements to determine the sizes to cut the book cover pieces. Be sure the zipper is long enough to go around three sides, and make the finished gusset/zipper loop about 1˝ longer than the measured periphery of the book.

Postcards

Finished size: 4″ × 6″

At 4″× 6″, a fabric postcard is a tiny quilt with big impact. It may stand alone as a mini art quilt, or it may include a greeting, quotation, Bible verse, or personalized message. It can travel *au naturel* or in a protective envelope. If you will be sending it through the mail, avoid loose pieces or embellishments that could be caught and/or torn in transit.

MATERIALS

- Photos, quotes, and messages
- 1 sheet pretreated inkjet fabric
- fast2fuse Double-Sided Fusible Stiff Interfacing: 1 piece, 4″ × 6″
- All-purpose sewing thread
- Hand-sewing supplies
- Buttons, beads, and specialty fibers

INSTRUCTIONS

1. Choose a photo that will size well to just under 4″ × 6″. This is the maximum space available on the front of the postcard for your altered images.

2. Use photo-editing software to position desired quotes or messages on top of the image for the postcard front (See Adding Text, page 30.) Position words for the postcard back on a blank 4″ × 6″ rectangle. For both sides, remember to allow ¼″ around the edges for satin stitching or other edge finishing.

3. Follow Steps 1–6 in the Basic Steps Summary (page 54), then cut out the front and back pieces separately.

4. Following the manufacturer's directions, fuse fast2fuse on the wrong side of the front piece.

5. Outline stitch each section of the image and then fill stitch with texture and color.

6. Position the back piece of the postcard and fuse in place.

7. Finish the edges with satin stitching done in rayon thread for a slight sheen.

8. Stitch embellishments in place securely—more securely than usual so they will survive their adventure through the postal system.

Greeting Cards

Is your heart so full it just won't all fit on a postcard? Consider a fabric greeting card. With four sides just waiting for printed images, stitched artwork, and embellishments, this format provides space for a well-composed message.

Finished size: 4″ × 5″

MATERIALS

- Photos, quotes, and messages
- 1 sheet pretreated inkjet fabric
- fast2fuse Double-Sided Fusible Stiff Interfacing: 2 pieces, 3¾″ × 4¾″
- Scrap fabrics for background
- 2 pieces muslin, 5″ × 8″
- Plain paper
- Buttons, beads, and charms
- All-purpose sewing thread
- Hand-sewing supplies

INSTRUCTIONS

1. Lay out the pages of your greeting card on paper. Plan a photo, quotation, wisecrack, or message for each of the four pages available.

back	front

inner left	inner right

2. Choose a vertical photo. Any photo that will cover the entire card should size well to just under 4″ × 5″. This is the maximum space available for your altered images on the pages of a standard size greeting card. You can, of course, make the card as large or as small as you like.

3. Use photo-editing software to position desired quotes or messages on top of or around the images (See Adding Text, page 30.) For all pages, remember to allow ¼″ around the edges for edge finishing and the center fold line.

4. Follow Steps 1–6 in the Basic Steps Summary (page 54) then cut out images for each page separately and set aside.

5. Any page that will not be covered completely by your photos should be covered by scraps. Experiment by overlaying scraps in a crazy-patch arrangement, or simply cover the entire surface. Trim the scraps even with the edge of the muslin.

6. Arrange the printed images on top of the finished muslin pieces. Stitch in place and fill stitch with texture and color.

7. Following the manufacturer's directions, fuse 2 pieces of fast2fuse to the wrong side of one muslin piece, leaving ¼″ between the pieces for the center "spine." Fuse the remaining piece of muslin on the opposite side, encasing the interfacing between the 2 muslin pieces.

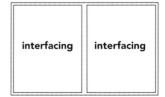

8. Use a straight stitch to sew through the center so the card will fold. Stitch around the edge through all the layers with a serger stitch or satin stitch to secure.

9. Stitch decorative fibers, ribbons, or trims around the outer edge with monofilament thread or decorative threads. Hand stitch buttons, beads, and baubles in place. Sign and date with a permanent marker.

Friendship Books

MATERIALS

- Photos, quotes, and messages
- 2 or 3 sheets pretreated inkjet fabric
- Muslin scraps: 4 pieces, 3" × 6"
- fast2fuse Double-Sided Fusible Stiff Interfacing: 4 pieces, 2¾" × 2¾"
- Fabric scraps: 8 pieces at least 3⅛" square
- Plain paper
- Gluestick
- Monofilament thread
- Specialty threads, as desired
- Hand-sewing supplies
- Buttons, beads, charms, or other embellishments
- Scraps of ribbon, textured fibers, and trims

Photo by Lori Marquette

Finished size: 3" × 3"

Whether your best friend lives next door or thousands of miles away, a miniature friendship book filled with funny photos and thoughtful messages will be a treasured gift!

INSTRUCTIONS

1. Lay out the pages of your friendship book by cutting four 3″ × 6″ pieces of notebook paper and stacking them. Use paper clips to clip together the top 2 pages and the bottom 2 pages. Fold all of the pages in half to create a book with 3″ × 3″ dimensions and write the page number on the outer corner of each page. This will be your planning book.

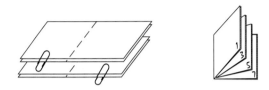

2. Choose photos that will size well to just under 3″ × 3″. This is the maximum space available on the pages for altered images.

3. Use photo-editing software to position desired quotes or messages on top of or around the images. For all pages, remember to allow ¼″ around the edges for edge finishing and the center fold line.

4. Follow Steps 1–3 in the Basic Steps Summary (page 54).

5. Cut the photos and words from your test print and arrange them on the planning book. Glue them in place so the page numbers are still visible. Separate the stacked pages. You'll notice the page numbers do not run consecutively. The page numbers should look like those in the diagrams below.

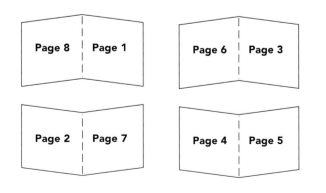

6. When you are satisfied with the composition, follow Steps 4–6 in the Basic Steps Summary.

7. Following the manufacturer's directions, fuse interfacing squares so they are centered on the wrong sides of muslin pages 8/1 and 6/3 (refer to the planning book). Be sure to leave the center "spine" area empty.

8. Arrange scrap fabric squares right side up on each of the muslin pieces so they overlap slightly in the center. These will be the page backgrounds, so refer to the planning book and arrange them accordingly. Baste in place. Trim the outer edges even with the muslin.

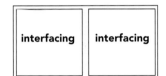

9. Position the fabric photos and words on each page. Stitch in place, using monofilament thread. Fill stitch with texture and color.

10. Place pages 8/1 and 2/7 together, wrong sides facing, and fuse. Do the same with pages 6/3 and 4/5. Stitch around the outer edges with straight or decorative stitches. Stitch on ribbons, trims, and fibers as edge finishing, if desired.

11. Stack the assembled pages to form the book and stitch down the center through all the layers with straight stitches.

12. Add embellishments by hand with a needle and thread. Sign and date with a permanent textile marker.

Pillow Shams

Finished size: 18″ × 24″

Create a memorable gift of a pillow sham with a photo of the recipient's own grandchild, child, best friend, cherished pet, or special moment printed on it. Especially nice for the person who has everything!

MATERIALS

- Photograph (horizontal orientation works best)
- 2 sheets pretreated inkjet fabric
- 1/3 yard fusible fleece
- 1/4 yard contrasting fabric for inner border
- 1 yard coordinating fabric for outer border and pillow back
- Sewing thread to coordinate with fabrics
- Monofilament thread
- Dark upholstery thread
- 2½ yards ruffle, fringe, or piping (optional edge trim)

CUTTING

From the fusible fleece, cut 1 piece, 10½″ × 16½″

From the inner border fabric, cut:

- 2 strips, 2″ × 16½″
- 2 strips, 2″ × 13½″

From the outer border/back fabric, cut:

- 1 strip (top border), 3½″ × 19½″
- 1 strip (bottom border), 2½″ × 19½″
- 2 strips (side borders), 3″ × 18½″
- 2 pieces (back), 18½″ × 14½″

INSTRUCTIONS

1. Choose a horizontal photo that will size well to just over 10″ × 16″. This is the maximum space available on the pillow sham for the altered image. Remember to allow 1/4″ around the edges for seam allowances.

2. Follow Steps 1–5 in the Basic Steps Summary (page 54), dividing the image into two 8″ × 10″ segments and printing each segment on a separate sheet of pretreated fabric. Stitch the segments together into one panel, press the seams open, rinse well if appropriate, and dry completely.

3. Following the manufacturer's directions, fuse fleece on the wrong side of the joined panel and fill stitch with texture and color. Square the edges of the finished panel to 10½″ × 16½″.

4. Stitch the top and bottom inner border strips to the photo panel, using 1/4″ seams. Stitch the side inner border strips to the panel.

5. Add the outer border strips in the same manner.

6. If you are using an edge trim, position it around the periphery of the pillow front with raw edges aligned. Baste in place.

7. Fold 1/4″ to the wrong side on one long edge of each back piece. Fold in another 1/4″ and stitch close to the first fold. Place the pillow front and back together with right sides facing so the hemmed edges overlap in the center. Pin in place.

8. Stitch around all sides, using a 1/4″ seam.

Tote Bags

Finished size: 18″ × 22″ × 5″

An oversize tote bag is a thing of beauty to a quilter! Space, glorious space! Space for fabric, space for threads, space for tools, rotary cutter, mat, and ruler—space for more fabric! With a little tweaking, this tote bag concept could be adapted as a diaper bag, too.

MATERIALS

- Photograph (horizontal orientation works best)
- 4 sheets pretreated inkjet fabric
- 1¼ yards (total) assorted fabrics for outside of tote
- 1⅛ yards lining fabric
- 3 yards 1″-wide belt webbing for handles
- 1 yard fusible fleece
- Sewing thread to coordinate with fabrics
- Monofilament thread
- Dark upholstery thread

CUTTING

From the tote fabric, cut:

- 2 front side borders, 3″ × 14½″
- 2 front top and bottom borders, 3″ × 23½″
- 1 back top section, 16¾″ × 23″
- 1 back bottom section, 2¾″ × 23″
- 2 sides, 6″ × 19″
- 1 bottom, 6″ × 23″

From the fusible fleece, cut:

- 1 front, 18″ × 22″
- 1 back, 18″ × 22″
- 2 sides, 5″ × 18″
- 1 bottom, 5″ × 22″

From the lining fabric, cut:

- 1 front, 19″ × 23″
- 1 back, 19″ × 23″
- 2 sides, 6″ × 19″
- 1 bottom, 6″ × 23″

INSTRUCTIONS

1. Choose a horizontal photo that will size well to just under 14″ × 18″. This is the maximum space available on the tote bag for the altered image. Remember to allow ¼″ around the edges for seam allowances.

2. Follow Steps 1–5 in the Basic Steps Summary (page 54), dividing the image into four 7″ × 9″ segments and printing each segment on a separate sheet of pretreated fabric. Stitch the segments together into one panel, press the seams open, rinse well, and dry completely.

3. Add the side borders, using a ¼″ seam allowance. Add the top border piece. *Do not add the bottom piece yet!*

4. Following the manufacturer's directions, fuse the front fleece piece to the wrong side of the photo panel, lining up the top edges. Avoid touching the fleece with the iron along the bottom, where the final border will be added. Fill stitch with texture and color.

5. Cut the webbing into 2 equal lengths. Position and pin one piece of webbing on the stitched front, as shown in the diagram, so the ends of the webbing extend 1″ past the bottom raw edge of the stitched front.

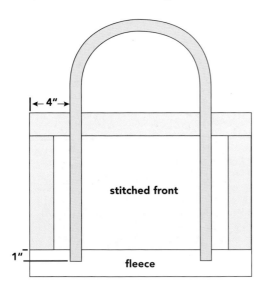

6. Starting at one end of the webbing, stitch along one side, ending 1″ below the top edge of the tote front with the needle down. Pivot and stitch across the webbing. Pivot again and stitch down the opposite side. Repeat to stitch the other end of the webbing piece to the tote front.

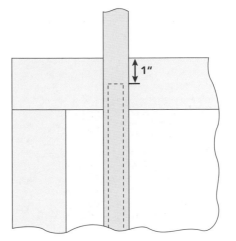

7. Complete the tote front by adding the final border strip across the bottom, stitching through the fleece and webbing. Press the bottom border to fuse the fleece in place. Trim the tote front to 19″ × 23″.

8. Following the manufacturer's directions, fuse the back fleece piece to the wrong side of the back top section, lining up the top edges. Avoid touching the fleece with the iron along the bottom, where the back bottom section will be added.

9. Pin the remaining piece of handle webbing on the back as you did on the front. Stitch along each side of the webbing as before.

10. Complete the tote back by adding the back bottom section, stitching through the fleece and webbing. Press to fuse the fleece in place.

11. Following the manufacturer's directions, fuse the fleece side pieces to the tote side pieces. Fuse the fleece bottom to the tote bottom. Stitch the bottom piece between 2 side pieces along their short ends, using a ½″ seam allowance. This will form the gusset.

side	bottom	side

12. Pin the gusset to the tote front along the sides and bottom, with right sides together. Stitch, using a ½" seam allowance and pivoting at the corners.

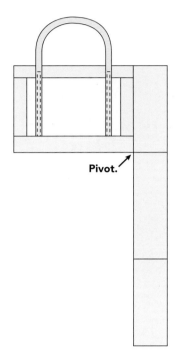

Pivot.

13. Pin and stitch the gusset to the tote back along the sides and bottom as you did on the front. This completes the outer shell of the tote bag. Leave the tote wrong side out.

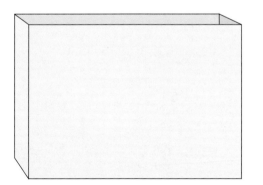

14. Stitch the bottom lining piece between the 2 side lining pieces along their short ends, using a ½" seam allowance to make the lining gusset.

15. Pin the lining gusset to the lining front along the sides and bottom, with right sides together. Stitch, using a ½" seam allowance and pivoting at the corners.

16. Pin and stitch the lining gusset to the lining back along the sides and bottom, leaving a 4" opening in the middle of one seam for turning.

17. Insert the lining inside the tote so the right sides are facing. Fold the handles toward the bottom to prevent them from getting caught in the stitching. Pin the lining to the tote along the top edge, matching the seams.

18. Stitch around the top edge, using a ½" seam allowance. Turn the bag right side out through the opening in the lining. Topstitch close to the top edge through all the layers for added strength. (Do not stitch through the handles.) Close the opening in the lining by hand.

19. With the tote right side out, flatten the bag and topstitch down one side of the front, stitching through the front and side, ⅝" from edge. Begin with a backstitch at the top edge of the tote and end with a backstitch ⅝" from the bottom edge. Repeat on the opposite side of the tote front. Repeat stitching, ⅝" from the bottom edge, beginning and ending with a backstitch ⅝" from either side.

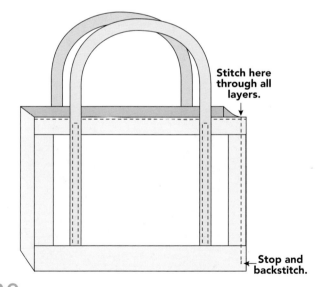

Stitch here through all layers.

Stop and backstitch.

20. Flatten the tote from the back side and repeat Step 19, topstitching along the sides and bottom.

21. Flatten the tote from the side and topstitch the bottom edge of the gusset in the same manner. Repeat on the opposite side gusset. This additional stitching helps the tote bag keep its shape while standing.

Pansies for My Sister,
20˝ × 16˝, 2006 by Pam DeWitt.

Photo by Lori Marquette

Bold Sojourn,
55″ × 36″ triptych, 2006
by Beth Wheeler and Lori
Marquette. When Beth and
Lori met a husband-and-wife
team selling honey and cut
sunflowers at their local
farmers' market, they quickly
arranged a visit to the
sunflower field.

Iris Fantasy,
29″ × 23″, 2006
by Beth Wheeler. Three blue-and-yellow irises with
touches of orange feature interesting shadows
created with hard lighting techniques.

Serendipity,
16″ × 20″, 2006
by Beth Wheeler. A bed of orange poppies beside a
country road caught Lori's eye, prompting a photo safari.

Toadshade,
24″ × 18″, 2006
by Susan A. Niehaus. This work
began as a digital photograph taken
in the woods on Susan's farm. The
leaf in the lower right corner is a
scan of an actual leaf.

A Study in Blue,
15″ × 13″, 2006
by Susan A. Niehaus. (In the private
collection of Mr. and Mrs. A. L. Augur.)
Susan's attention to detail shows in
the heavy stitching and hand beading.

Continuity,
24″ × 32″, 2006
by Beth Wheeler and Lori Marquette.
Afternoon light created blue shadows
on this partially open rose. Saturation
and hue adjustments allowed the colors
to be enhanced, and stitching empha-
sized the light playing on the petals.

Photo by Lori Marquette

Photo by Lori Marquette

Quiet Anticipation,
24″ × 32″, 2006
by Beth Wheeler and Lori Marquette.
The startling depth of this piece is
deepened by careful thread selection.

Photo by Lori Marquette

Inner Vortex,
30″ × 40″, 2005
by Beth Wheeler and Lori Marquette. To direct the eye to the tightly whorled center of a pink rose, Lori cropped the image tightly and altered the colors, adding orange to the petals and purple to the shadows.

Photo by Lori Marquette

Tranquility,
24″ × 32″, 2006
by Beth Wheeler and Lori Marquette. A photo safari to a spring bulb show offered daffodils, tulips, and lush cyclamen just waiting to be photographed. The pink cyclamen were particularly shy and kept turning their faces away from the camera. Threads in many shades of pink add to the complex texture.

Photo by Beth Wheeler

Pondering Translucency,
30″ × 40″, 2006
by Beth Wheeler. The contrast between the stark white petals and deep purple throat of a spring pansy is caught by the camera. Careful cropping guides the eye, while bold purple, yellow, and metallic white threads emphasize the color and texture.

Indigo Bliss,
24″ × 32″, 2006
by Beth Wheeler. Opulent blossoms on a delphinium display shading in blues and purples, enhanced with saturation adjustments and many shades of blue and purple threads.

Abundance,
16″ × 20″, 2006
by Beth Wheeler and Lori Marquette. Filtering and adjustments in contrast and saturation exaggerate the shading on the petals of these yellow-and-orange tulips.

Labyrinth of Love,
16″ × 12″, 2006
by Beth Wheeler and Lori Marquette. (In the private collection of Mr. and Mrs. David Gorrell.) Shadows and highlights created by light falling on a rose with many layers of petals increase the illusion of depth.

Serenity,
30″ × 40″, 2005
by Beth Wheeler. Zooming in on the iris's throat eliminates distracting background, increases the abstraction of this piece, and spotlights the filter's added texture.

Clarity,
30″ × 40″, 2005
by Beth Wheeler and Lori Marquette. Deep shadows created by hard lighting are usually avoided by photographers; however, they work in our technique by creating drama and depth.

Red Bluff Red Rock Canyon,
16″ × 20″, 2006
by Beth Wheeler. Landscape compositions require less filter abstraction.

Innocence,
16″ × 20″, 2006
by Beth Wheeler and Lori
Marquette. The ruffled cup of
an unusual daffodil variety
made outlining a challenge.
Once again, the outline map
saves the day!

Photo by: Lori Marquette

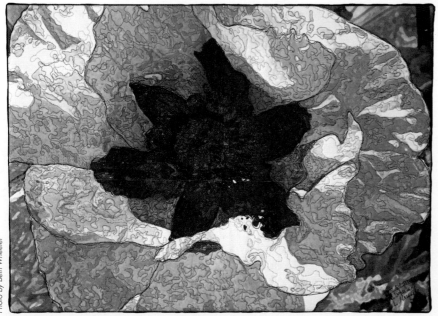

Photo by Beth Wheeler

Balance,
20″ × 16″, 2006
by Beth Wheeler. A snapshot of a
peach poppy taken in a courtyard in
Santa Fe required selective filtering to
hold the detail in the purple throat.

Beckoning,
30″ × 40″, 2006
by Beth Wheeler. As you work with our techniques,
you'll begin to look at flowers, buildings, statues,
lighting, sky conditions, and other phenomena in
a new way. Gladiolas have never been a favorite
flower of Beth's, and yet this year she suddenly
noticed the captivating texture of the leaves,
petals, and stamens.

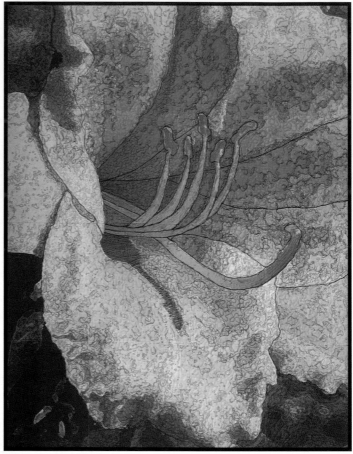

Photo by Beth Wheeler

Photo by Beth Wheeler

***Three Graces from the Garden
of the Gods, Colorado,***
16″ × 20″, 2006
by Beth Wheeler.

Traditions,
16″ × 20″, 2006
by Beth Wheeler. (In the private
collection of Cheryl Elser.) Normally
a photo of a fading rose would not
be desirable, but our combination of
filtering, printing, and quilting uses
the variation in the colors of the
petals to add texture and interest.

Photo by Beth Wheeler

Photo by Lori Marquette

Desert Rose,
30″ × 40″, 2006
by Beth Wheeler
and Lori Marquette.

Photo by Lori Marquette

Silhouette,
16″ × 20″, 2006
by Beth Wheeler and Lori Marquette.

Photo by Lori Marquette

Nicholas,
16″ × 20″, 2006
by Beth Wheeler and Lori Marquette.

The Apitz Home,
20″ × 16″, 2006
by Beth Wheeler
and Lori Marquette.

Original photo by Claudia Claussen. Quilt photo by Lori Marquette.

sources & resources

For a list of other fine books from C&T Publishing, ask for a free catalog:

C&T Publishing, Inc.

P.O. Box 1456

Lafayette, CA 94549

(800) 284-1114

Email: ctinfo@ctpub.com

Website: www.ctpub.com

For quilting supplies:

Cotton Patch Mail Order

1025 Brown Ave.

Lafayette, CA 94549

(800) 835-4418

(925) 283-7883

Email: CottonPa@aol.com

Website: www.quiltusa.com

Note: Fabrics used in the quilts shown may not be currently available; fabric manufacturers keep most fabrics in print for only a short time.

MEDIA SERVICES

C&T Publishing's professional photography is now available to the public. Visit us at www.ctmediaservices.com

PHOTO-EDITING SOFTWARE

Adobe Photoshop Elements

Adobe Photoshop Creative Suite (CS)

Adobe Systems Incorporated

www.adobe.com

Free 30-day trial versions of Adobe's outstanding software packages, such as Photoshop Elements, Photoshop CS, Illustrator, Acrobat, and others.

Tutorials and free downloadable plug-ins, such as Kaleidoscope V1, used in the Kaleidoscope Star quilt on page 23.

CorelDRAW

Corel Corporation

www.corel.com

Publisher of Paint Shop Pro; offers a free 30-day trial version and a full download for a reasonable price

Kaleidoscope Kreator 2.0

Kaleidoscope Collections, LLC

www.kalcollections.com

The software package is available both as a CD option or a download.

Sketch Master

Redfield Plugins

www.redfieldplugins.com

Special effects for graphic designers.

SHAREWARE AND FREEWARE

Searchable sites for free trials of popular software:
www.allianceweb.sk
www.soft32.com
www.winplanet.com

Freeware and shareware for Mac and PC. Search on kaleidoscope, fractals, or anything else that tickles your creative-fancy bone!

www.download.com

A free download of photo-editing software, including edge effects:

www.photoelf.com

A wonderful site for shareware. Includes consumer ratings and popularity ratings.

www.snapfiles.com

This is the site for Kaleider software. The trial version is free and the registered version is very affordable (PC only).

www.whizical.com

PRETREATED INKJET FABRICS

Bubble Jet Set 2000 and Bubble Jet Set Rinse

www.cjenkinscompany.com

Color Plus Inkjet Fabrics

www.colortextiles.com

Crafter's Images PhotoFabric and artwork CDs. (These are the author's favorites!)

www.createforless.com

E.Q. Printables

www.electricquilt.com

Ink and continuous ink systems for inkjet printers

www.inksupply.com

June Tailor Colorfast

www.junetailor.com

Printed Treasures by Milliken

www.printedtreasures.com

WEARABLE-ART PATTERNS

www.designandsew.com
www.junecolburn.com
www.kaylakennington.com
www.parkbenchpatterns.com
www.rag-merchant.com

THREAD

American & Efird, Inc.

www.amefird.com

Signature variegated trilobal polyester thread

Coats & Clark

www.coatsandclark.com

Upholstery thread. Spools have only 150 yards on them, so plan accordingly!

Linda Palaisy

www.lindapalaisy.ca

Variegated 100% cotton hand-dyed thread. Don't let the cost fool you—it comes in 1,000-yard spools!

Red Rock Threads

www.redrockthreads.com

Discount source for many of the threads used in this book.

Sulky

www.sulky.com

Variegated 12-weight, 30-weight, and 40-weight threads in cotton, rayon, and/or polyester

Valdani Threads

www.valdani.com

Hand-dyed (variegated) cotton thread. We especially like the 30-weight.

YLI

www.ylicorp.com

Variegated machine-quilting thread

PHOTOGRAPHIC IMAGES IN QUILTS

Blending Photos with Fabric, Mary Ellen Krantz and Cheryl Hayes, The Electric Quilt Company, 2004

Fabric Photos, Marjorie Croner, Interweave Press, 1990.

Fun Photo Quilts, Ami Simms, Mallery Press, 1999.

Memory Quilts in the Making (For the Love of Quilting) from Inc. Leisure Arts, Oxmoor House, 1999.

More Photo Fun, Cyndy Lyle Rymer and Lynn Koolish, C&T Publishing, 2005.

Photo Fun, Cyndy Lyle Rymer and Lynn Koolish, C&T Publishing, 2004.

Photo Transfer Handbook: Snap it, Print it, Stitch it!, Jean Ray Laury, C&T Publishing, 1999.

Quilting More Memories: Creating Projects with Image Transfers, Sandy Bonsib, Martingale & Company, 2001.

Simply Amazing Quilted Photography, Tammie Bowser, Bowser Publications/Mosaic Quilt Studio, 2002.

MACHINE TECHNIQUES

Coloring with Thread, Ann Fahl, C&T Publishing, 2005.

Creative Machine Stitching: Special Effects for Quilts and More, Patricia Nelson, That Patchwork Place, 2003.

Simple Thread Painting: Quilt Savvy, Nancy Prince, American Quilter's Society, 2004.

COMPUTER TECHNIQUES

Creative Computer Tools for Artists: Using Software to Develop Drawings and Paintings, Joann Lawrence Pollard, Watson-Guptil, 2002.

The Designer's Guide to Astounding Photoshop Effects, Steven Heller and Gail Anderson, How Design Books, 2004.

Digital Art Studio: Techniques for Combining Inkjet Printing with Traditional Art Materials, Karin Schminke, Dorothy Simpson Krause, Bonnie Pierce Lhotka, Watson-Guptil, 2004.

Mastering Digital Printing, Harald Johnson, Course Technology PTR, 2004.

DIGITAL PHOTOGRAPHY TECHNIQUES

Creative Photo Printmaking, Theresa Airey and Michael J. McNamara, Amphoto Books, 1996.

Digital Abstract and Macro Photography, Ken Milburn, Course Technology PTR, 2005.

Start with a Digital Camera, John Odam, Peachpit Press, 2003.

Fine Art Nature Photography: Advanced Techniques and the Creative Process, Tony Sweet, Stackpole Books, 2002.

CREATIVITY AND INSPIRATION

Art and Fear, David Bayles and Ted Orland, Image Continuum Press, 2001.

The Artist's Way, Julia Cameron, Tarcher, 2002.

The Creative Call: An Artist's Response to the Way of the Spirit, Janice Elsheimer, Shaw, 2001.

It Was Good: Making Art to the Glory of God, edited by Ned Bustard and Sandra Bowden, Square Halo Books, 2000.

Sacramental Living: Falling Stars & Coloring Outside the Lines, Dwight W. Vogel and Linda J. Vogel, Upper Room Books, 1999.

The Vein of Gold, Julia Cameron, Tarcher, 1997.

Walking on Water: Reflections on Faith and Art, Madeleine L'Engle, Shaw, 2001.

MAKING SENSE OF LIFE

A Beginner's Guide to Constructing the Universe: Mathematical Archetypes of Nature, Art, and Science, Michael S. Schneider, Harper Paperbacks, 1995.

about the authors

Beth Wheeler, aka "Muttonhead" (right), is a free-lance artist, product-development specialist, author, and teacher. In the past sixteen years, she has written more than 44 books for sewing, quilting, craft, and collecting audiences; written hundreds of articles for trade and consumer publications; and published her own line of Muttonhead quilting patterns and products. Beth has been a crafter since age five and a quilter since age sixteen. She credits her mother and maternal grandmother with inspiration and introduction to early techniques—and access to a Singer featherweight!

A passion for discovery led her to develop processes for the analysis of technique and design. These skills are the basis for her classes, workshops, articles, books, and products.

Beth lives in northern Indiana with husband, Geoffrey; son, Jake; and dogs, Kippy and Sydney, in a house happily crowded with a jumble of fabrics, computers, printers, projects in progress, and treasured stuff too precious to actually use.

Lori Marquette, aka "Sassy" (left), is a freelance artist, product development specialist, and certified massage therapist. She has worked with Beth, providing balance and marketing her designs, for sixteen years. During this time, Lori has renewed her childhood appreciation for quilting and crafting gained from the many hours spent watching her grandmother hand quilt and embroider as she was growing up.

She brings a lifelong passion for the healing arts, a unique perspective, and a healthy sense of adventure to artistic creativity. This facilitates therapeutic persuasion in her technique and design. It is a privilege for her to share this energy with you.

Lori lives in northern Indiana with her sons, Tyler and Ryan; and toy poodle, Cody.

We are blessed and we are grateful!

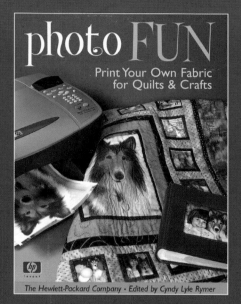
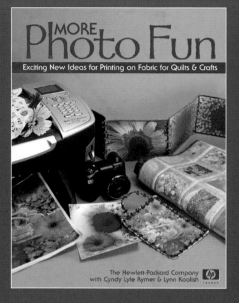
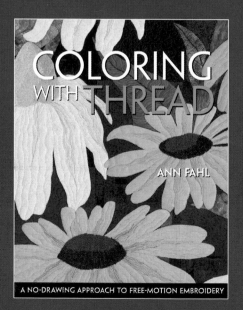
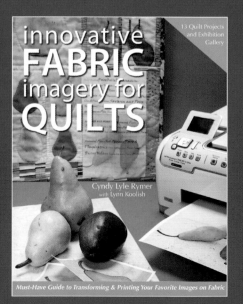